Innocence Blues

Rebecca Winn

BookLeaf
Publishing

India | USA | UK

Presentation by *BookLeaf Publishing*

Web: www.bookleafpub.com

E-mail: info@bookleafpub.com

ISBN: 9789358311389

First edition 2023

ACKNOWLEDGEMENT

Thank you to my sister, Emily that pushed me to write this book. If it weren't for our late-night talks, this book wouldn't exist. Thank you to my professor, Mr. Bittorf that helped me get comfortable sharing my work. If it weren't for your help, I never would've shared my writing, let alone put it in a book. Thank you to all the friends, coworkers, and family that let me read them these poems as I wrote them. You all supported me when I needed it the most as I questioned this book and challenge.

Miracle Mornings

Dried flowers on a countertop,
Music blaring from a stereo,
A scent identical to a coffee shop,
Sunlight playing in the window.

Nothing more than serenity and the scent of
coffee in the air
Dizzy dancing in the kitchen
The sense of euphoria is everywhere.
It almost feels like fiction–

But that is the moment that I'll know that I've
done it right.

The Language of Nightmares

Simple words on a page, rhymes and rhythms.
Baloney and blether to some,
Yet still to others these rhymes and rhythms
reveal their nightmares of reality
These words attest to the horrors they've
persisted through.

These words represent every evening I've cried
on my own, waiting for the sandman to take me.
They are every step I've taken, every inch I've
crawled, and every breath I've taken.
These simple words, or blether to some, are the
reason I stand before you
The reason that for every fall I've taken, I still
climb and carry on

These words rip my shelter away from me
They throw me into a pit of nightmares I swore
I'd forget
They force me to relive the horrors in my mind
And yet, they are the reason I'm still alive.

Scripted Existence

I'm lost…
I'm lost in a way that I'm no longer wandering
In a way that I'm no longer blooming with the
spring flowers
I'm no longer recognizing the reflection that
stares back at me.

I tried–
I tried to follow your path
To follow the life written for me
The life that was supposed to make everyone
proud
That was supposed to be perfect for me.

But here I am…
Here I am running away from it
Running away from the little girl that wanted to
be just like you
The little girl that always believed you
That always ran to you when she was scared and
smiled when you were near.

If I hadn't lived it…I'm not sure I'd believe you
if you told me that she and I were the same.
That her innocent smile had grown into– me.

Little Grown Girl

I'm not her.
I'm not the girl that smiles all the time
I'm not the girl in the pretty sundress
I'm not the girl that always puts words to her
feelings out loud.
I'm not her.

I'm not that little girl anymore.
I'm not the little girl that talks to everyone
anymore
I'm not the little girl that always needs her
momma
I'm not the little girl that always needs her dad.
I'm not that little girl.

I may not be that little girl anymore.
I may not be that girl from the stories,
But I am a human being.

I'm a human being learning.
Learning how to cope
Learning who I am without everyone else
Learning what kind of person I want to be.
I'm learning how to go from being that little
girl–

To being grown up.

I'm the girl that likes to paint
That loves to read but can't help but finish that
TV show.
I'm the girl that can't live without music
That loves tattoos and eyeliner.
I'm that girl.

I'm the girl no one expected me to be.
I'm learning how to heal that little girl–
And how to be a person they could be proud of.

Teenage Dejection

From temporary cartoon tattoos to permanent
ink under the skin,
From bedtime stories to lonely late-night
laments,
From loving learning to being drained by
lectures–
How can we not feel as though we've lost
ourselves?

While we grieve the children we used to be, it
feels as though no one can see–
Like mountains hiding the sun, we've covered
the care for what's been done.

We pretend it's okay
We pretend that we don't dread our entire life
unfolding
We pretend like we know what we're doing.
But the reality of life smashes into us day and
night.

We argue with our parents while our mind
pursues its own civil war.
We speak in hopes of finally being heard
We change in hopes of finally being seen

Sometimes parents forget how much pressure
there is–
All just by being a teen.

Society's Children

Skeleton hands grasping black sands
Souls lost in the hourglass
Screaming for air with liquid lungs
Carnival mirrors locked in their senses

Ayúdame.
Ayúdame. Please ayúdame.

Within the walls, the deceitfully innocent cancer
grows
Pitch-black air nurturing lies and masking scars
Rope wrapped around limbs
A still silent day burning their skin

Ayúdanos. Please ayúdanos.

Young minds trapped in a generation's tar not
knowing who they are
Lost in the hourglass
Stuck in carnival mirrors
We children scream with liquid lungs
Our last traces are our skeleton hands grasping
black sands.

Ayúdanos.

Blue.

Did you know that I love the color blue?

The color blue is like love; in that, it came out of
nowhere.
I wasn't looking for a new favorite color–
In fact, I was done with colors altogether.

Then there was a blue crayon just right there
In the box of tattered pencils, markers, and
crayons.

The next thing I knew,
I couldn't get enough of you– blue I mean…
Blue
Blue
Blue.

Blissful, beautiful, brilliant…blue.

Dear Old Healing

Dear healing,
Where are you, old friend?
Have you forgotten me again?

You know how dear you are to me
Will you please come back again?
I know you must be vexed by now–
Every time you turn; I need you "once more."

Though this feels more give than take
I need you to know how much I appreciate it.

You've helped me stand, old friend.
You've made me feel strong again.
I know that without you, I'd never make it.

Dear old healing,
I cannot thank you enough–
One day I will try
By taking delight in a simple breath

I may even, finally–
Let you turn around.

People Pleaser 101

I'm sorry–
Oh, I'm sorry–
I'm so so sorry.

What for, child?

Well…it seemed like I was in the way.
The way you looked at me felt like I had done
something–

Oh child, rest with ease.
Rest knowing you've done nothing wrong.
Rest knowing you are loved
Knowing that the simple fact that you breathe is
a miracle.

But I don't ever say the right things
Or guess the right answer
Or always know things I should

Child, you learn as you live.
You grow with your mistakes
Mistakes aren't to be shamed.
You aren't to be shamed.
Child, rest knowing that you are doing it right.

Chronic Insomniac

00:53
Can't sleep
Can't sleep
Can't sleep

Just be normal.
Sleep. It's not that hard.

What's wrong with you?
Why don't you just SLEEP?

It's all in your head, just turn off the screens and
sleep like everyone else.

God, I wish I could–
But you see, these screens aren't the problem
The problem is every single word running
through my mind

Every argument, every task still left to do
Every wrong word I've spoken in the last 18
years
Everything that seems to be wrong with me.

So no, I can't sleep. No matter how exhausted I
am.
I can't just drift peacefully with all the chaos in
my mind.
I can't sleep with every regret trapped inside
I can't sleep knowing how ridiculous I seem.

I just can't sleep knowing that…
I'm never going to be the way I used to be.

Depression Club

I can't help but feel it.
Feel the anxiety welling up inside me
Feel the depression creeping up a bit
No matter how hard I try to break free.

I can't help but see it.
The patterns that I keep trying to break
No matter how hard I strive, I just can't quit
All the hobbies and tasks just make me feel fake.

All the distractions and routines I build-up
The reminders and alarms still go off in my head
I guess that it's all part of the depression club
All parts of the anxiety spread

Medication, therapy, and therapist after therapist
It all runs back to me after the best days
Because in the nighttime, it all becomes
unrepressed
I wish I could go back to before I felt this
depression haze.

Household Government

Fallen angels
Losing all their grace
Banished to hell for stepping out of line

Gates to hold them in
Or even to keep them out
One judge, jury, and executioner.

Scary, right?
But what if I told it to you this way:

Lost teenagers
Losing themselves in the voices of the world
Grounded because they had to eventually
explode

Locked doors to hold them in place
And even locked doors to keep their favorite
people out
One, maybe two authorities–
I'll give you a hint…
In no way is it a democracy.

Friday Night Fright

It grabs you by the throat
Shakes your limbs with its mind
Shocks your heart into a thumping rhythm

Stomach-churning
Adrenaline rushing through your veins

There's no outrunning it
And if you let it,
It'll take your mind too.

Infectious Games

I love you–
But we can't right now

I love you–
But I need some time

I love you–
But only for right now.

You see, you're only a stepping stone
You're only here because I'm lonely
You're only enough until I find better.

You're good enough to hold
But not enough to really see my life

You're beautiful–
And I'll give you hope
I'll tell you "You're it for me"
"You're the girl for me"

I'll accidentally ask you to move in
But when I find better…
Well, that's it.

It's just hope and games
Because you see, you were just a page for me
While I tricked you into writing a book about
me.

Sincerely,
All the relationships of my generation

Neglected Expression

I need your comfort
I need your love
I need your time
Can't you just give it to me?
Just this once, please…

I'll do everything right
Please just tell me you're proud of me.

Let me know that I'm doing it right when I feel
like I'm doing it all wrong in your eyes…

Love by the Minute

I'm not ready yet
I can't hear the answers

I'm not ready because you were my first
The first one I wanted to meet my momma
That I told my dad about

The first one that made me focus on me
You were the only one that talked our issues out
You were the first that was okay with the word
"no"

You were the first that made me feel truly
beautiful–
That made me feel heard,
Seen,
Loved.

You were the only one I did things for, in spite
of what I felt.
In spite of the fear I stayed
In spite of the wounds still healing, I still
showed them to you
In spite of all my issues–
I allowed myself to love you.

To stay with you,
To dream of a future with you
To want you in my life

I finally felt whole–
And then, it all disappeared in a matter of
minutes.

Quality-of-Life

White coats and sterile floors
Bright lights and coffee pours

Almost as foreign as "normality"
Sometimes I forget that it's my reality.

I forget that I've been offered a place
That I earned my spot in this space

If not, then what was it all for?
Why did I survive its greedy hold twice,
If not for my place on this floor?
There must be some offset for that price.

Kind regards,
A cancer survivor and cancer researcher in
training.

Rippling Effects

Two weeks, and years of progress down the
drain.
At the same time, there's been progress made

Hard to speak up for myself
My mission is to please everyone else
Anxiety shoots up as the walls close in
I can't handle the noise,
These walls are paper thin.

Earbuds 'round my neck
Nothing but the music in my ear

Tension in the workplace and an unknown
roommate
Can't bring myself to talk to anyone but myself

But hey, at least…
At least I cook for myself
At least I have a routine
At least I can talk to myself
At least these pages ripple with the feelings
trapped within.

False Faces

It's getting hot in here
It's getting harder to breathe
How am I supposed to love myself when it feels
like everything is wrong?

How am I supposed to be happy in a room full
of people that would easily leave me behind?
People that would walk away without a single
thought about me.
That don't care if I made it home safe
Or if my head's in a good place

People that smile and nod like they care about
me
But won't ask me about my day
People that only check in with me when it feels
like an obligation
People that don't care to get to know me besides
what I write in my poetry.

How am I supposed to be okay surrounded by all
these false faces?

What if?

Two words haunt me in the nighttime.
Two simple words.
On their own, they don't mean much–
But when they are put together, they can control
your mind.

What if?

What if I had said this instead of that?
What if I had seen that?
What if I had known that?
What if I had done that instead?
What if this had happened?
What if this didn't happen?

What if…
It's a question that I can't answer
Most of the time, we'll never know.

What if haunts my entire being in the nighttime–
And sometimes, it controls me for days.
Sometimes I let it control me for days.

"What if," simply needs to be put to bed.
Like Pi, we'll never know how it ends.

Why should we suffer with a question, that will
not yield an answer?

Why do we question rather than take the leap in
the first place?

Opposite Day

The moonlight cries as it watches mere mortals
die
The same mortals the malignant sun scowls
upon
Sitting in the present tide watching the green
waves roll by
Listening to the blue grass in the summer sky
Strolling through life, taking it all in stride
because nothing fazes the powers held inside

But what if I told you everything you know is all
a lie?

What if the moon isn't morning and the sun isn't
smiling?
What if the water isn't blue and the grass isn't
green?
What if the grass doesn't grow from the ground
and the clouds don't rule the skies?

What if we are all terrified inside?